TRUE
Style

ISBN 0-439-68690-3

12 11 10 9 8 7 6 5 4 3 2 1   4 5 6 7 8 9/0

Printed in the U.S.A.

First printing, September 2004

BOOK DESIGN BY JENNIFER RINALDI WINDAU

Perfect World

TRUE Style

by **LAURIE CALKHOVEN**

Illustrated by **ANGELA MARTINI**

Scholastic Inc.

New York   Toronto   London   Auckland   Sydney
Mexico City   New Delhi   Hong Kong   Buenos Aires

CONTENTS

INTRODUCTION:

DISCOVERING YOUR *True Style*

Grab your BFF (Best Friend Forever)

and get ready for some fun!

Whether you're looking for ways

to change your hair

or boost your grades,

redo your room

or organize your locker,

these pages are packed

with smart advice and ideas

for looking great, feeling great,

and being an even

better you!

BEAUTY STYLE:

MAKE OVER YOUR *Look*

We know you're beautiful just the way you are, but there's nothing more fun than trying out new hairstyles or having an at-home spa party. Read on for tips, tricks, and beauty secrets.

Healthy Beauty

The healthier you are, the healthier you look. The real key to healthy hair, sparkling eyes, and glowing skin is eating a healthy diet, drinking lots of water, getting a good night's sleep, and remembering to exercise.

FOOD

Eat a diet with plenty of protein (foods like meat, fish, cheese, and nuts) and lots of fresh fruits and vegetables (at least five servings a day). Go easy on the chips and cookies after school—munch on an

Beauty Secret: GO TO THE MARKET WITH YOUR MOM OR DAD AND LOOK AT ALL THE EXOTIC FRUITS AND VEGETABLES YOU'VE NEVER TRIED. TASTE ONE NEW ONE EACH WEEK.

apple instead. And don't forget healthy whole grains, like wheat instead of white bread, and high-fiber cereals instead of sugary sweet breakfast mixes. Calcium (found in milk, cheese, and yogurt) is super important for healthy bones and teeth.

Healthy food doesn't just make you look more beautiful, it makes you smarter, too! Check out the Student Style chapter on page 42 for more "food for thought."

EXERCISE

Regular exercise not only keeps your heart pumping and your energy level up, it improves your blood circulation and sends all those good, healthy nutrients you're eating to your skin and hair.

Exercise can be fun—have a dance party after school, try out for a sports team, or even start a walking club with your BFFs.

REST

All that healthy food and exercise will have you looking great, but to really look and feel your best, you need your beauty sleep. Aim for ten hours a night. You will wake up full of energy and ready to start the day.

Starring You!
THE RIGHT HAIRSTYLE TO FRAME YOUR FACE

Whether it's short or long, straight or curly, hair is the one accessory we take everywhere. Look in a mirror and compare your face to the shapes below to find your best style. Having trouble figuring out which look is yours? Your BFF will be happy to help.

OVAL: Oval face shapes have even features, with the forehead and chin in proportion to each other. If this is your face shape, then lucky you. You can wear your hair just about any way you want. Long or short, one length or lots of layers—any style looks good on you. And with this face shape, you can pull off any kind of bangs.

HEART-SHAPED: Heart-shaped faces get narrower below the cheekbones, ending in a pointier chin. Hairstyles fuller around the ends will make your chin look wider. Short hair looks great on you. If you want to keep your hair longer, layers in the front can make your face look more oval. Heart-shaped faces look cute with any style of bangs.

ROUND: If you have full cheeks, then chances are you have a round face. Lots of layers and fullness on top with sleek sides can make round cheeks look narrower. Hair should be either shorter or longer than chin-length, and a side part will have you looking your best. Keep bangs on the long side with some face-framing layers.

SQUARE: Square faces usually have a broad forehead and cheekbones and a strong, square chin. Hair that's chin-length with layers that hug the face can slim those broad lines. Long, wispy bangs, cut even longer at the sides, will soften your forehead and make your eyes stand out.

Beauty Secret: WANT A NEW LOOK? GO THROUGH MAGAZINES TO FIND PICTURES OF CUTS YOU THINK MIGHT LOOK GOOD ON YOU. THEN TALK IT OVER WITH YOUR MOM, YOUR BFF, AND A HAIRSTYLIST TO FIND OUT FOR SURE IF THE CUT WILL WORK WITH YOUR HAIR TYPE. THEN GO FOR IT!

Thick or Thin, Straight or Curly?
HAIR CARE ADVICE

No matter what your hairstyle, you want your hair to look its best. Read on for some super hair dos and don'ts.

Wet

Washing your hair seems like a no-brainer, right? Who doesn't know how to do that? But most girls use too much shampoo. A quarter-size amount is enough. And be sure to use your fingertips—not your fingernails—to massage your scalp and work the suds through.

To condition or not to condition? The answer to that question depends a lot on your hair. Conditioners keep thick hair soft, but can weigh thin hair down. Girls with thin hair should con- centrate conditioners on the ends instead of on the roots, or skip it altogether. Curly hair can be dry, so using conditioner every time is a must.

FRESH
MAYO
CREAMY

> **Beauty Secret:** HALF A CUP OF WARM OLIVE OIL MASSAGED INTO DRY HAIR IS A GREAT INTENSIVE CONDITIONING TREATMENT. LEAVE IT IN FOR THIRTY MINUTES (YOU CAN CATCH UP ON SOME READING), THEN SHAMPOO. MAYONNAISE WORKS, TOO. GIRLS WITH THICK AND CURLY HAIR CAN DO THIS ONCE A MONTH FOR SOFT AND SMOOTH HAIR.

If you have thin, fine hair, chances are you have knots. Take a wide-toothed comb into the shower with you and use it to unsnarl your hair right after you apply conditioner. Never brush knots out of wet or dry hair; always use a comb.

Dry

Blow-dryers can dry out hair, so remember these tips: Never dry dripping-wet hair; first let it air dry for a while. Always keep your dryer moving and six inches away from your hair. Otherwise you may either "burn" it or risk drying it out.

Styling products can help you get the look you want. Leave-in conditioners and gels help curls hold their shape,

and volumizing sprays on the roots (never the ends) of thin hair can give it a lift.

The best way to find out what works for you? Experiment! And don't forget to share and compare styling tips with your friends.

honey shampoo

Ponytails!
NEW TWISTS ON CLASSIC STYLES

Nothing's easier than pulling your hair into a ponytail. Keep an extra scrunchy and colorful elastics (always use the kind that won't snag or tear your hair) in your backpack in case you want to pull your hair back for a spur-of-the-moment kickball game or some heavy-duty homework. Having trouble making a braid? Just ask your BFF for help with these cool new styles.

PONYTAIL FLIP TWIST:

First make a low ponytail at the base of your head (where your head meets the top of your neck) with an elastic.

Then reach up under the ponytail and use your fingers to make a hole in the middle of your hair right above the elastic.

With your other hand, twist the tail and bring it up so that the fingers that are making the hole can grab the ponytail and pull it through. Presto! Ponytail Flip Twist.

PONYTAIL WRAP:

First make a low ponytail at the base of your head with an elastic, leaving a one-inch piece of hair under the tail outside of the elastic.

Wrap the loose hair around the elastic two or three times.

Pull the rest of the strand into the elastic under the ponytail. Try this with pigtails, too!

PIGTAIL LOOPS: Make low pigtails on each side of your head and tie off with elastics. Make a loop and pull hair halfway through the elastics a second time.

PIGTAIL PRETTY:

Is your hair too short for a ponytail? Try little pigtails all over your head. You'll need smaller elastics for this style. Or how about two high pigtails—gathered on each side of your head? They are super cute with short, curly hair.

BRAID BASICS: Make small braids on either side of your face for a framing effect. Or, braid small sections of hair on the crown of your head before pulling it all back into a ponytail. And for a fancier look, knot the center of a ribbon around a section of hair and then braid, using the ribbon as one of your three sections.

THE RIPPLE EFFECT: Create curls

while you sleep. Before bed, wet your hair thoroughly (not sopping wet!) and make braids all over your head, braiding as close to the ends of your hair as you can. When you wake up the next morning, remove the elastics and finger-comb your hair! Before you start, remember to think about how big you want your ripples to be—the smaller the braid, the more ripples you'll get.

PINS AND CLIPS: Don't forget to shine.

Jazz up your style with all kinds of sparkly, shiny accessories. Pretty bobby pins and barrettes are great for keeping hair off your face. Clips come in all kinds of cool styles and sizes—from little ones to decorate your whole head to one big clip to hold up all of your hair! Make sure to twist your hair before you pin or clip it for the best hold.

Sleepover Spa Fun
BEAUTY TIPS FOR YOUR NEXT
ALL-NIGHT PARTY!

Have you ever dreamed of going to a day spa with your BFFs? Believe it or not, you don't even have to leave home (or spend all your allowance) to become beautiful! Gather all your beauty products together and invite your BFFs for a spa sleepover. Experiment with new hairstyles, try out new fashion looks, and pamper each other with manicures and pedicures. And don't forget your favorite CDs for the all-important background music for atmosphere!

Face

This Oatmeal-Honey Facial Mask is the mask to use when you want more beautiful skin. Just try not to giggle too much while you wait to rinse it off!

In a bowl, mix three tablespoons of regular, uncooked oatmeal flakes with two tablespoons of honey and enough milk to make a thick paste. Apply to your face, making sure to keep it away from your mouth and your eyes.

The skin around these areas is especially delicate, and face masks can be too harsh. Leave on for ten minutes and rinse with warm water. Your skin will be softer and smoother.

> **Beauty Secret:** THE BEST WAY TO KEEP YOUR SKIN LOOKING HEALTHY IS TO USE SUNSCREEN—NOT JUST WHEN YOU'RE AT THE BEACH OR HANGING BY THE POOL, BUT WHENEVER YOU'RE OUTSIDE. PROTECTING YOUR SKIN AGAINST THE SUN "TODAY" WILL HELP YOU TO HAVE YOUNGER-LOOKING SKIN "TOMORROW."

Hands and Feet

Being nice to your nails with manis and pedis is never more fun than when you and your BFFs do the pampering. You'll need emery boards for filing and shaping, a nailbrush to scrub away the dirt, lotion to soften your hands and feet, nail polish remover, cotton balls, and last but not least, polish in lots of fun colors!

Add toe separators to your list if you're planning on doing pedis, too.

Start by taking off any old nail polish with polish remover and a cotton ball, then wash your hands and nails. Trim your nails to your desired length and shape them with an emery board.

Soaking your hands and feet in warm, soapy water for five minutes cleans and moistens your nails. Then it's time to brush out any gunk that's still underneath. Use a washcloth to gently push the cuticle back from the nail on each finger.

Beauty Secret: TRY NEW COLORS, OR PAINT EACH NAIL A DIFFERENT COLOR. TINY STICKERS, MADE ESPECIALLY FOR NAILS, ARE LOTS OF FUN, TOO.

Finish with moisturizing lotion and once it's absorbed into your skin and nails, break out the polish.

For perfect polish, start with a clear base or protective coat. Then paint a strip of polish onto the middle of the nail. Next paint a strip on either side to coat the nail. Let the polish dry for about five minutes before applying the second coat. A clear top coat protects the color and makes your nails shine.

FASHION STYLE:
MAKE OVER YOUR *Closet*

Are you trendy or sporty, stylish or girly, or
a little bit of each? Discover your true fashion
self and give your closet a cool makeover.

Pop Quiz:
WHAT'S YOUR FASHION STYLE?

When it comes to fashion, are you bold and trendy
or soft and casual? Totally sporty or super girly?
Take this quiz to discover your inner fashionista.

1. My favorite shoes are

   a. cool new motorcycle boots.

   b. ballet slippers.

   c. sneakers.

   d. cute, pointy Mary Janes.

2. My favorite PJs are

   a. a bright blue tank top and matching capri pants.

   b. flannel PJs in a dreamy cloud pattern.

   c. a big T-shirt.

   d. a pink nightgown and fuzzy pink slippers.

3. My BFF wants a T-shirt for her birthday.

   a. I go to my favorite store in the mall and pick out the coolest one they have.

   b. I design a one-of-a-kind T-shirt using fabric paints and her favorite artist as inspiration.

   c. I find a T-shirt that features the name and number of her favorite sports star.

   d. I look for one in a pretty color with a nice flower design on the front.

4. My favorite hair accessory is

   a. a butterfly clip.

   b. multicolored scrunchies.

   c. nothing at all.

   d. a velvet headband.

5. The hairstyle I like best is

   a. whatever is new and "in."

   b. a French braid.

   c. short and easy.

   d. long and curly.

6. Out of these colors, I would choose

   a. outrageous orange.

   b. lovely lavender.

   c. lime green.

   d. pretty pink.

7. My favorite accessory is

   a. my cool new watch, just like the one in this month's magazine!

   b. my long, skinny, striped scarf.

   c. Does a tennis racket count?

   d. my prettiest matching necklace and earrings.

I answered

Mostly As: **TRENDY GIRL**. I share the same fashion sense as the latest stars. I love bright, bold colors, and my BFFs trust me to clue them in to the coolest new trends.

Mostly Bs: **STYLE GIRL**. I have the style of an artist and choose colors and clothes to match. I love putting together outfits, and always choose just the right accessories.

Mostly Cs: **SPORTY GIRL**. I love being active and can't sit still! Comfort is more important to me than style. I want to be free to kick a soccer ball or make a basket.

Mostly Ds: **GIRLY GIRL**. I love sweet, frilly, and pretty clothes. I look for details like ribbons, ruffles, and flowery prints, and I can't get enough of pink.

Closet Makeover

Are you a girly girl with a closet full of jeans, or a trendy girl stuck in last year's fashions? Now that you've uncovered your inner fashionista, it's time to give your wardrobe a makeover.

Make a space for three piles.

Keepers: Clothes you love, clothes that fit, fashions that don't look left over from a trend two years ago.

Maybes: Clothes you're a little tired of, but still fit and are in good shape. Read on for tips for turning last year's fashions into this year's styles.

Gotta Go's: Be brutal. Anything that doesn't fit is simply taking up valuable closet space. That sweater with the grape juice stain all over the stomach can go right in the

> **Fashion Secret:** ANYTHING YOU HAVEN'T WORN IN MORE THAN A YEAR IS READY FOR THE GOTTA GO PILE.

trash, but the rest of it can be boxed up for charity or for your little sis.

Now take a look at what's left and make a list of what you need to dress in style. Read on for cool tips and tricks to turn your Maybes into Keepers.

New Looks for
Last Year's Clothes
GET CREATIVE

Take a look at your Maybe pile. Want to dress up some of those tired fashions? Head to your local crafts store for ideas and inspiration.

Go through the bargain bins and look for funky buttons. Sew new ones on last year's denim jacket for a fab new look. Run a line of glittery star, sun, and moon buttons down the side seams of last year's jeans, or replace the buttons on a pretty blouse.

Fashion Secret: REMEMBER, THE BUTTONS DON'T HAVE TO MATCH. FIND FUN COLORS, OR GO WITH AN ANIMAL THEME.

Silk Flowers can be attached to your clothes with safety pins—big flowers look great on belts, tops, jackets, and even baseball caps. And glue them to your flip-flops. Or glue cute little silk flowers around the collar of a T-shirt or up and down the front—like a row of buttons.

Don't forget the paint aisle. Brighten up your old T-shirts with fabric paint. Come up with your own one-of-a-kind design or copy a picture from a book or magazine.

> ## Fashion Secret:
> ARE YOUR PANTS OR SKIRTS TOO SHORT, BUT FIT EVERYWHERE ELSE? ADD FUNKY FABRIC OR A RUFFLE TO THE HEM TO CREATE A WHOLE NEW LOOK. USE LEFT-OVER FABRIC FOR A MATCHING BELT OR HEADBAND.

Use your computer to print out your favorite picture of you and your BFFs, or your name in big, bold letters onto iron-on transfer paper. Create cool new T-shirts for you and your BFFs!

Whatever you do, remember to have fun and **BE CREATIVE!** Why not gather together all your buttons, flowers, and paints and invite your friends over for a Design-Your-Own-T-Shirt party?

Turn those jeans you love (but you've outgrown) into **SUPER-CUTE CAPRI PANTS.** Here's how:

First try on your jeans and have your BFF mark them with chalk to the length you like. Use a ruler to make sure the chalk line is straight.

Then lay the jeans flat on the floor and, with a pair of heavy-duty scissors, cut them straight across where they're marked.

Now add your own personal touch. Take extra ribbon or your favorite fabric (leopard spots, anyone?) and measure around the hem of the jeans pant leg. Cut the correct amount of fabric and pin it around the hem.

Ask an adult to help you either iron on (with adhesive bonding tape) or sew the fabric to the bottom of your jeans.

Have fun wearing your jazzy new capris!

PUTTING IT ALL TOGETHER

Accessories can turn a boring old outfit into the funkiest new trend. Don't forget to add shine and sparkle to your outfits with cool earrings, bracelets, hair clips, hats, and scarves. And don't be afraid to mix them up— wear three or four bracelets on one wrist, or two necklaces that look cute together.

Now go back to the closet. Only this time, make it

> ## *Fashion Secret:*
>
> ACCESSORIES ARE GREAT FUN, BUT THE COST ADDS UP. WHY NOT CREATE AN "ACCESSORY SWAP" WITH YOUR SISTERS OR EVEN YOUR BFFS. MAKE A LIST OF ALL YOUR FUN JEWELRY, SCARVES, BAGS, AND HAIR CLIPS AND SHARE THE WEALTH. REMEMBER TO KEEP YOUR ABSOLUTE FAVES—LIKE THE EARRINGS YOUR FAVORITE AUNT GAVE YOU—OFF THE LIST AND IN YOUR OWN PRIVATE STASH.

Mom and Dad's (remember to ask permission first). Your dad's old ties make great belts and headbands and even straps for shoulder bags.

Mom's scarves can be fun, too. Wrap one around your neck for an instant fashion update, or tie it around your waist for a fab new belt. Big square scarves, folded on the diagonal, can even be wrapped around pants and skirts for a vintage look.

And don't forget to add your unique creative touch to your accessories. Decorate with animal stickers or glue pretty little buttons on big plastic bracelets and barrettes. Buy lots of beads and make your own bracelets and necklaces, and glue animal appliqués to your backpack.

Whatever you do, express yourself.

Fashion Secret:
VINTAGE AND CONSIGNMENT SHOPS
ARE GREAT PLACES TO FIND CHEAP,
FUNKY JEWELRY.

Shop Like an Expert

Now that you've made room in your closet by giving away all those clothes that don't fit, it might be time for a little shopping trip. Here are some fab shopping tips.

AT HOME

Know what you have. Already own three pairs of jeans? You probably don't need another. But maybe you need a cute new skirt.

Know what you want. Flip through your favorite magazines and catalogs; check out the girls at school. Decide ahead of time what you need to fill out your wardrobe, and bring your list.

OUT AND ABOUT

Try everything on. And don't forget to move around in it and make sure it's comfortable. There's nothing worse than getting home with a great new top only to discover it strangles you at the neck.

Stay in your budget. If your mom's willing to spend thirty dollars, don't beg for more.

Beware of trends! Some come and go in only a couple of weeks. Go easy—start with accessories while you wait to see if the fad will last.

ROOM STYLE:

MAKE OVER YOUR *Room*

What better place to express your style than in your own room? Whether you want to totally redecorate or just update the pictures on your wall, these tips will give your bedroom a shot of style that makes it yours.

Planning

WHAT YOU NEED TO DO BEFORE YOU MAKE THE BIG CHANGE

Want to create a room that says you? It all begins with imagination, creativity, and planning—not to mention your parents' permission!

Are you a sports fan but have bunnies all over your walls from nursery school days? Or an animal lover stuck with flowered wallpaper? Maybe you have lots of collections with no place to show them off, or so much clutter everything gets lost.

> ### Decorating Secret:
> DO YOU LIKE ALL YOUR STUFF, BUT STILL WANT TO MAKE A CHANGE? MOVE IT AROUND. PUT YOUR DESK UNDER THE WINDOW AND MOVE YOUR BED TO THE OPPOSITE WALL. YOUR ROOM WILL FEEL BRAND-NEW.

It all starts with brainstorming. Make a list of all the stuff you like and would never, ever get rid of—

that picture of you riding your favorite horse, or the baby blanket your grandmother knitted for you.

Then list the things you'd like to toss: a boring bedspread; dull posters; or a rug with a big hot chocolate stain.

Next, think about what you use your room for. Is it a secret little nook where you hide away for quiet reading or study time, or do you love hanging out in your room with your BFFs, blasting your CDs after school? Do you want your room to be comfortable and cozy, or bright and funky?

Once you've answered all those questions, think about the ways you can express your style and read on for some simple ways to make your room say *you*!

> ## Decorating Secret:
>
> IF YOU WANT TO MAKE BIG CHANGES, LIKE REARRANGING FURNITURE, MAKE A SKETCH FIRST. YOU'LL WANT TO BE SURE YOU'RE GOING TO LIKE YOUR NEW FLOOR PLAN BEFORE YOU START MOVING AROUND HEAVY FURNITURE.

Lights, Color, Action!

Changing the lighting or adding color are easy ways to add new spark to your old "crib."

Want to create a cozy atmosphere? Turn off that overhead light and use small indirect lights instead (be sure to have at least one good lamp in your reading and study space). Put a cute paper lantern over an old fixture, or tack string lights around your window frame or your mirror.

Painting is the biggest change you can make to your room—and it doesn't have to be expensive.

> **Decorating Secret:** NOT SURE ABOUT THAT NEW COLOR? PAINT ONE WALL AND LIVE WITH IT FOR A FEW DAYS. IT'S EASIER TO REPAINT ONE WALL THAN YOUR WHOLE ROOM IF YOU FIND YOU DON'T LOVE IT. OR MAYBE JUST USE THE NEW COLOR FOR ONE OR TWO WALLS.

Which colors do you love? Having a hard time choosing? What's your favorite season? Which crayon in your crayon box always gets used first? Would you rather be swimming in the ocean or hiking in the mountains? These are clues to which color will make you happiest in your room.

Be careful not to choose a color that will clash with your favorite picture or the new bedspread you just picked out.

Get creative. Wide stripes in two shades of the same color create instant panache! Do you love rainbows? How about painting one on your wall? Or draw a zoo scene if you love animals. Sketch your design on the wall in pencil and then fill in the lines.

Painting is never more fun than when you have a painting party. Invite your BFFs over in their oldest clothes, turn on the music, and have a blast. Reward everyone with pizza and ice cream afterward, and offer to return the favor.

Decorating Secret:

THE KEY TO A GOOD PAINT JOB IS PREPARATION! COVER YOUR FLOORS AND FURNITURE WITH AN OLD SHEET. PUT MASKING TAPE AROUND WINDOWS, DOOR FRAMES, AND ANYTHING ELSE YOU DON'T WANT TO GET PAINT ON (SUCH AS THE CEILING WHERE IT MEETS THE WALL). IF CLIMBING LADDERS IS NECESSARY, MAKE SURE YOU HAVE ADULT SUPERVISION.

Spruce Up Your Space

Sometimes your room just needs a "space lift."
Here are some inexpensive and easy ways to
spruce up your place.

SEW fun and funky buttons on old pillows.

CREATE an iron-on transfer design (a picture of your pet?) for your pillowcases.

DECORATE picture frames with seashells collected at the beach, or different bottle caps.

PAINT an old lamp shade with fabric paint and glue a ruffle to the bottom.

GLUE silk flower petals, ribbons, or buttons onto your lamp shade.

PUNCH tiny holes in a dark blue lamp shade. It'll look like stars in the night sky!

HANG ceiling-to-floor strings of beads or curtains around your bed or a comfy reading chair to create a secret nook.

TRADE bedspreads with your sister, or your BFF.

BUY a fake-fur rug for next to your bed. It'll be the first thing your tootsies touch every morning.

DECORATE your headboard with paint or stickers.

PAINT sayings like "You're a Star," "You Rock!" and "You Go, Girl!" on the frame around your mirror.

TRIM a pretty postcard to size, cut a hole in the middle, and glue it onto your light switch.

USE cute hair clips for curtain tiebacks.

> # Decorating Secret:
> GO "SHOPPING" IN YOUR ATTIC. IS THERE
> A COOL OLD LAMP YOU COULD PAINT OR
> A TABLE THAT WOULD BE THE PERFECT
> PLACE FOR HOMEWORK? YOU CAN USE
> OLD SOFA PILLOWS TO CREATE
> A LOUNGING AREA ON THE FLOOR.

Storage is super important if you want to keep your space free of clutter. Do you have lots of collections? Shelves are great places to display dolls, stuffed animals, sports trophies, CDs, and your favorite books. Storage bins keep toys, out-of-season clothes, and craft supplies organized and out from under your feet. Choose bright colors that go with your color scheme or stash them in the closet.

Decorating Secret: DON'T WANT TO SPEND YOUR
HARD-EARNED ALLOWANCE ON PLASTIC STORAGE BINS? ASK FOR
STURDY CARDBOARD BOXES AT THE SUPERMARKET (THE ONES
THEY'RE GOING TO THROW AWAY). AND SHOE BOXES ARE GREAT FOR
YOUR SMALLER TREASURES. PAINT THEM OR COVER THEM IN PRETTY
WRAPPING PAPER TO STOW YOUR STUFF IN STYLE!

Picture-perfect

Another quick and easy way to create a room that
says *you* is to change what's on your walls! Read on
for some ideas, and make a list of your own!

BUY INEXPENSIVE FRAMES AT THE
DISCOUNT STORE AND FILL THEM WITH COLORFUL
WRAPPING PAPER IN A JAZZY DESIGN.

DO YOU LOVE YOUR OLD CAMP T-SHIRT, BUT IT
DOESN'T FIT ANYMORE? CENTER THE LOGO OVER A
PIECE OF CARDBOARD AND POP IT INTO A FRAME.

PASTE PICTURES OF ALL YOUR FRIENDS ON
A PIECE OF POSTER BOARD AND HAVE
THEM WRITE MESSAGES TO YOU IN COLORED
MARKERS—INSTANT ART.

CREATE A COLLAGE OF YOUR FAVORITE THINGS—
PICTURES, FALL LEAVES, BIRD FEATHERS—AND
HANG IT UP ON YOUR WALL.

COVER A PIECE OF CORKBOARD WITH
PRETTY FABRIC FOR A COOL ONE-OF-A-KIND
BULLETIN BOARD.

GET MESSY! CREATE AN ABSTRACT "MASTERPIECE"
FOR YOUR WALL—FINGER PAINTING IS FINE—AND
SIGN YOUR NAME IN BIG LETTERS!

Keeping It You!
COMBATING CLUTTER

The real key to keeping your room neat and free of clutter is to clean up a little every day. It's very tempting at the end of a long, busy day or a marathon homework session to just drop your clothes on the floor. But that pile has a weird habit of growing, and the next thing you know, you have a mountain of dirty clothes and nothing to wear.

If you don't have a hamper, get one.

Carry your empty water glasses and snack dishes to the kitchen on your way to breakfast in the morning.

Put a box in your dresser drawer and use it as a catchall for hair clips and scrunchies.

Clear a spot on your desk for school books and papers.

Plastic storage bins or stacked cardboard boxes are great places to keep things like craft supplies, souvenirs, and sports equipment.

Make a habit of spending five to ten minutes a day—before or after school—picking up your clutter, and your room will always be neat.

Make cleaning fun. Remember Mary Poppins? No matter how neat you are, you'll still have to do a major cleaning once in a while—things like dusting, sweeping, vacuuming, and organizing. Turn on the music and dance your way to clean. Or challenge your brothers and sisters to a clean-off. Whoever finishes first gets their other chores done for them that day!

Two's Company
SHARED ROOMS THAT STILL SAY YOU

Lots of girls share a bedroom with their sisters. Here are some fun ways to make sure you're happy roommates.

Make sure each of you has an area to call your own, with your own pictures, calendars, and other things to hang on matching bulletin boards.

Does your sister like ballerina posters, while you want to gaze at sports stars? Matching frames can pull the two looks together.

Feeling squeezed out of the closet? Hang a big silk flower or tie a ribbon to divide the closet in half, and then stick to your own sides.

Decorating Secret: DOES YOUR SISTER WANT A PINK COMFORTER, BUT YOU PREFER GREEN? LOOK FOR A RUG OR CURTAINS THAT INCLUDE BOTH COLORS.

Combat clutter with two big baskets—one for each of you. And when you find each other's things lying around, toss them in the baskets, not at each other!

Even sharing a room, you can still create your own space. As long as you're imaginative and have fun, there's a solution to every design dilemma.

STUDENT STYLE:

MAKE OVER YOUR *School Style*

Follow these tips and tricks to have fun, stay organized, and make your school year rock.

Pop Quiz:
WHAT'S MY STUDENT STYLE?

1. My teacher gives a homework assignment. I
   a. take careful notes and ask questions if I don't understand everything.
   b. plan to call my BFF after school to get the details.

2. When the bell rings at the end of the day, I
   a. make sure I have everything I need in my backpack before leaving school.
   b. dash off to cheerleading practice and hope that I can get into the classroom later to get my stuff.

3. I'm working on a group history project with three other kids. When it's time to divide up the work, I

   a. volunteer to be project leader and do the research no one else wants to do.

   b. scrunch down in my seat and hope no one notices me.

4. My favorite place to sit in the classroom is

   a. the front row, where I can see and hear everything.

   b. next to my BFF—it's easier to pass notes that way.

5. My big math test is tomorrow. I

   a. review my notes and get a good night's sleep. I'm prepared.

   b. planned to study, but my favorite TV show was on, and then I had to call my BFF.

I answered

MOSTLY A◊. I'm ready to do my best. I'm organized and willing to take notes, ask questions, and do my share of the work on group projects. But I need to add some fun to my busy schedule.

MOSTLY B◊. I'm trying. But when it comes to hitting the books, I kind of get sidetracked. I need to stop those negative habits before they take over. If I get organized, I'll have time to do it all.

Brain Food

Do you find yourself snoozing through social studies, or propping open your eyelids after lunch? When you eat and what you eat are super important when it comes to staying awake and remaining alert throughout the day.

BREAKFAST

Mom was right when she said breakfast is the most important meal of the day. Start with protein to boost your energy—healthy cereal with milk, peanut butter on whole wheat toast, or eggs are all good choices to get your day started right.

If you're scheduled for late lunch this year, pack some snacks in your backpack for a mid-morning munch. Energy bars, dried fruit, raisins, or baby carrots are all things you can eat in the halls, between classes.

LUNCH

Try to eat lunch no later than six hours after you have breakfast. Mix your proteins (chicken, fish, cheese) with starches and vegetables for a real energy burst. Avoid high-sugar foods. They can give you quick energy, but watch out for that "sugar crash." You'll be more tired than ever.

Fruit is a good choice when you're craving something sweet for an after-school snack. Celery with peanut butter or cream cheese (combining a vegetable with a protein), or peanut butter on a crunchy apple will give you energy when it's time to do homework or practice your dance moves.

DINNER

Eat dinner before eight at night, and combine proteins, starches, and vegetables just as you did at lunch. Before dinner, go over what you had to eat that day. Were you short on vegetables? Then load up on the "green stuff!"

Okay, you've been healthy all day. You deserve dessert. The natural ingredients in milk and ice cream are proven to make you sleepy. So dish up a few scoops, but don't eat right before you go to bed.

Locked Up
ORGANIZE AND DECORATE YOUR LOCKER AND BACKPACK

Do you sit down in math only to realize you forgot your book or your pencil? Is your English notebook in your locker when it's time to take notes on the book report due next week?

When it comes to staying on top of things at school, a little organization goes a long way. You can't make any permanent changes to your locker, so how do you make it reflect your style? With magnets, of course!

Get a magnetic mirror and hang it up inside your locker door at eye level. Glue little magnets on the backs of things that will make you happy to open your locker every morning—party invites, notes from your BFFs, magazine pics of your favorite celebs.

> **Study Secret:** WRAP A SHOE BOX IN PRETTY PAPER AND FILL IT WITH EMERGENCY AND SCHOOL SUPPLIES—EXTRA ELASTICS AND SCRUNCHIES FOR YOUR HAIR, SAFETY PINS, PENS, SCISSORS, AND TAPE.

Keep your books organized and your notebooks clearly labeled, so you don't wind up in math with your English notebook and in science with your social studies project.

Take a few minutes to clean out your locker every week or so.

Backpacks need to be organized, too. Try to clean yours out every day, when you finish your homework. Recycle unneeded papers. Update your calendar or assignment book. Slip your homework papers into a folder. And make sure your pens, pencils, and eraser are in their own compartment or in a zip-up pencil case. Leave space for lunch and snacks that you'll pack in the morning.

> **Style Tip:** DOES YOUR BACKPACK LOOK JUST LIKE YOUR BFF'S? EXPRESS YOUR OWN STYLE BY GLUING ON A BUTTERFLY APPLIQUÉ OR BY WRITING YOUR NAME IN FABRIC PAINT.

Homework Help
TIPS TO KEEP YOU AT THE
HEAD OF THE CLASS

One of the best ways to stay on top of homework is to be organized. Write down all your assignments and make the most of your time. If you tackle the hardest subjects first, the rest will seem like a piece of cake.

Do you have soccer practice after school? A dentist appointment this week? Try to make the best of little bits of time. You and your friends can quiz each other at the bus stop. Read over your math problems in the dentist's office. Tackle half of this week's vocabulary list in the fifteen minutes between tap and ballet.

> ***Study Secret:*** STUDY AFTER SCHOOL (AT HOME OR AT THE LIBRARY), RATHER THAN AFTER DINNER, SO YOU HAVE PLENTY OF TIME AND WON'T GET OVERTIRED. AN AWAKE BRAIN REMEMBERS MORE THAN A SLEEPY ONE!

One of the best places to study is at home. If you organize a homework zone in your room, sitting down to study will be a lot easier. Make sure you have good lighting, a comfortable chair, and lots of room for your books and papers. Try to keep the distractions, like TV and phone calls, to a minimum.

Experiment! Some girls learn best with music playing in the background. Others need total silence. Maybe you can study only in short spans—like fifteen minutes at a time—before you need to get up and move around.

Break big projects down into smaller pieces. Get out your calendar and work backward from the project's due date, assigning yourself a task for each day.

> **Study Secret:** WHEN YOU'RE FEELING STUCK, SLOW DOWN AND TAKE A BREAK. DO SOME JUMPING JACKS, TAKE SOME DEEP BREATHS, AND THEN TACKLE WHATEVER IT IS AGAIN, MORE SLOWLY. STILL STUCK? ASK YOUR PARENTS, TEACHERS, OR FRIENDS FOR HELP.

And don't forget to have fun. Write jokes and songs to help you remember facts. Write silly sentences about your spelling words, dance or race around the house in between subjects.

Test Matters
TIPS FOR TAKING TESTS AND GIVING PRESENTATIONS

Does the idea of a test or the words "oral report" make the butterflies in your stomach start fluttering like crazy? Read on for tips on staying cool the next time you hear the word "exam."

Test Tips

Be prepared. Start studying for a test at least a week ahead. If you think it will help (and you can keep the giggling down), form a study group with your friends. And don't forget to visit the library—one of the best study spots.

Review your notes and get a good night's sleep the night before a test. Don't skip breakfast or lunch—kids who eat a healthy breakfast do better on tests.

At the start of the test, relax and take a deep breath. Read the directions carefully and don't be afraid to ask a question if you don't understand something.

Test Secret: SKIP OVER QUESTIONS YOU CAN'T ANSWER RIGHT AWAY. GO BACK TO THEM LATER.

Read all of the questions and answers carefully. If there's time, proofread your answers before turning in your paper.

Polished Reports and Presentations

Begin by choosing a topic that really interests you. Are you excited about horses or stars? Find a way to make the project exciting for you.

Once you have a subject, write down as many questions as you can think of about your topic. Which ones can you answer for your presentation? And which ones need more research?

Go beyond the usual sources—books, magazines, encyclopedias—for your research. Surf the net or interview people who know a lot about your topic.

Study Secret: FOR WINNING ORAL REPORTS, BE SURE TO PRACTICE, PRACTICE, PRACTICE. THE BETTER YOU KNOW YOUR MATERIAL, THE MORE CONFIDENT YOU'LL FEEL. DON'T FORGET TO SMILE AND MAKE EYE CONTACT WITH YOUR AUDIENCE.

Once you've answered all your questions, it's time to organize your paper. Think about your topic and about how one fact leads to another. Soon you'll have an outline for your report.

Capture your teacher's attention right away with a strong opening—use an interesting fact or quote and state your main points. Then use details and examples to back up your opening remarks.

Having Fun!

School isn't just about hard work and homework. It's also about making friends, joining clubs, trying new things, and having fun.

Don't get so wrapped up in worrying about math and science that you forget about your artsy side, or the part of you that wants to do something for your community. Sign up for an art class, try out for the school play, or grab an instrument and join the band. Volunteer at the animal shelter or brighten lives of senior citizens at a nursing home.

Is there something you've been dying to learn—like knitting or photography—that isn't offered at your school? Call your local community center and see if there's someone who's willing to teach and start a new club.

Are sports your thing? Going out for a team can be scary, but if you're willing to play hard, you'll have the right attitude to make the team. Focus on learning the game and having fun.

When are clubs and sports too much of a good thing? When you don't have time left for yourself. Remember that you need time for homework and to hang out with your friends.

Fun Secret: MAKING NEW FRIENDS DOESN'T HAVE TO BE HARD, ESPECIALLY WHEN YOU GET INVOLVED WITH SOMETHING YOU LOVE TO DO. YOU'LL MEET PEOPLE WHO SHARE YOUR INTERESTS. REMEMBER TO SMILE AND BE YOURSELF.

Make a list of everything you have going on. Is it too much? What's most important to you? If going to Girl Scouts or to cheerleading practice starts to feel overwhelming, then it may be time for some time management. Talk over your schedule with your parents or your older sister first.

Your talents are just waiting to be discovered. Keep trying new things until you find the ones you love!

SELF STYLE:
MAKE OVER *You*

Every girl has something she wishes she were better at. Do you want to be a better sister, friend, or daughter? Do you want to learn Spanish, bowling, or knitting?

Think big. Believe that you can make a difference and go for it!

Brainstorming
WHAT DO YOU WANT TO BE BETTER AT?

Quick—don't think. Write down the three things that make you happiest.

1. _____

2. _____

3. _____

Quick—don't think. Write down three things you'd like to have more of—friends, good grades, or awesome dance moves.

1. _____

2. _____

3. _____

Quick—don't think. Write down the three things you daydream most about (e.g. getting the lead in the school play or being invited to more parties).

1. _____

2. _____

3. _____

What do your answers say about you? Do you love spending time with your little sis, but have so many after-school activities that you're always pressed for family time? Do you dream about getting great grades, but never crack open a book? Do you want to make new friends, but feel too shy to talk to new people?

Make a short list of things you want to achieve, then do just one thing every day to help make your dreams come true. It can be as small as cleaning your room, or as big as starting a new club at school.

Whatever your goals—be the best you.

Five Ways to Get What You Want

1. KNOW WHAT YOU WANT.

Do you want to plan the best sleepover ever, start a babysitting business, or get straight As on your next report card? Knowing what you want helps you to get it.

2. TAKE SMALL STEPS.

Do you have a big goal, like dancing a solo at your ballet recital or getting an A on your reptiles report? Make a list of everything you need to do to achieve your goal, such as mastering the grand plié or learning everything there is to know about turtles. Concentrate on checking things off your list rather than trying to do everything at once.

3. DON'T GIVE UP TOO SOON.

You know that boring old saying, "If at first you don't succeed, try, try again?" It's true. Don't let mistakes make you feel you'll never reach your goal—learn from them and move on.

4. ASK FOR HELP.

Does it feel like learning Spanish is always going to be really, really hard? Ask your teacher for extra help. You could also start a study group, or ask your friends to write their notes to you in Spanish. Maybe you even have a classmate who's a Spanish whiz and could use help in your best subject. There are lots of ways to ask for help and have fun or make new friends while you're at it.

5. SMILE!

Everything sure seems easier when you have a smile on your face.

Make a Difference

Volunteering is a great way to make the world a better place. It's guaranteed to make you feel good, and you'll have a lot of fun along the way. Here are just a few things you might want to try. Don't forget to write down some brilliant ideas of your own.

Do you and your BFFs love animals? Volunteer your time at the local Humane Society or the ASPCA, where homeless animals need love and attention —not to mention good homes.

Organize a Park Clean-up Day. First check with your local town hall. Then grab your BFFs, some garbage bags, and a pair of gloves, and get an adult

---

Caring Secret: VOLUNTEERING CAN BE AS BIG AS ORGANIZING A GARAGE SALE WITH ALL THE PROFITS GOING TO CHARITY OR AS SMALL AS TAKING A NEIGHBOR'S DOG FOR A WALK. WHATEVER YOU DO, REMEMBER, YOU DO MAKE A DIFFERENCE.

---

to drive you to the local park. **Pick up litter**, empty cartons and cups, newspapers, and anything else that doesn't belong. Recycle whatever you can.

Tutor a student who's having trouble in a class that you ace. Added bonus—you'll make a new friend.

Volunteer to visit senior citizens at the local nursing home. Not only do they have lots of interesting stories about "the olden days," they love getting visitors, too. You can even ask to run a bingo game or to help in other organized activities.

Team up with your best friend and **volunteer to read** to the little kids at your local library or at the children's ward in the local hospital. Choose a book you loved when you were little, and you and your BFF can act out the parts together.

MY VOLUNTEERING IDEAS

1._____

2._____

3._____

TOTAL STYLE

Style is more than fashion, beauty, and good grades. It's an attitude. It's about being the best girl you can be. And most of all, it's about doing what you love and being happy. Write down your own style secrets here, and share them with your BFFs.

My Style Secrets

_____

_____

_____

_____

_____

_____

_____

_____

_____

_____

My BFF's Style Secrets

_____

_____

_____

_____

_____

_____

_____

_____

_____

_____

_____

_____

_____